# MODEL SOLDIERS

## ARMIES IN MINIATURE

*With an introduction by Massimo Alberini*

**CRESCENT BOOKS**

# Contents

3 Foreword
5 Toys and collectors' items
From historical figurines to tin soldiers
8 Plastic and single models
12 Paper soldiers
13 Showcases and dioramas
14 The war game

All the photographs in this volume are by Carlo Bevilacqua, with the exception of the following: plates 12, 13, 21, 22, 30, 44–7, 51, 54, 66–72, 79, 87, 88, 94–6, 104, 106, 107, 109, 110 (Philip Stearns); plates 3–6 (F. A. Mella); plates 25, 53, 55 (Norman Newton Ltd); plates 102, 103, 105 (Historex Agents). The black and white drawings in the introductory pages were provided by CBG

*Translated from the Italian of Massimo Alberini*

The author would like to express his gratitude to Brigadier Peter Young, military historian and veteran wargamer; to Mr Philip Stearns, expert photographer of military miniatures, of whose work there are many splendid examples among the colour illustrations; to Lieutenant-Colonel J. B. R. Nicholson, Editor of *Tradition* magazine; to Edward Surén of 'Willie' Figures; and to Mr Lynn Sangster of Historex Agents. Their expertise, offered so generously, contributed greatly to this book.

The author would also like to thank all those who, with their assistance during his travels, made his task of collecting information so much easier. He is particularly grateful to Dr Anna Maria Bonucci of the San Martino Museum, Vomero, Naples; the officials of the Army Museum in Madrid; the curator of the *Musée de l'Armée,* Paris; the Administrative Staff of the Kinstgewerbe Museum, Cologne, and of the Arsenal Museum, Vienna; the President of *Sabretache*, Paris; the Kober Company, Vienna; CBG Mignot, Paris; the Testi Family, Padua; Dr Osvaldo Campassi of San Damiano d'Asti; the Imagerie Pellerin, Epinal; the President of the San Marciano Academy, Turin; Vincente Julio, Madrid; Colonel Gasparinetti, the Secretary of the Italian Collectors' Union, Rome.

In Milan the author would like to thank Mr Telomei of the Austerlitz Group; Dr Giancarlo Zipoli, President of the Italian Club of Military Models; Commendatore Noé, the Mastro Gepetto Company; Gianni Tura, Maurizio Boverio, Anacleto Carrera, and above all Dr Renato Artesi who made the Author free of the treasures of his collection and of his vast experience as a collector.
**Massimo Alberini**

# Toys and collectors' items

The idea of an adult collecting 'toys' like model soldiers strikes many people as absurd. This view is completely mistaken. Far from being a childish pursuit, an interest in model soldiers reflects a deeper concern with history.

Furthermore, the collecting urge, whether it be for model soldiers, stamps or exotic bric-a-brac, stems from the very human characteristic of desiring – and displaying – the rare and the unusual. This is most in evidence if the treasured object has been made by a skilled craftsman and represents luxury and riches. This has happened particularly with dolls and reached its highest level with automata and the first mechanical toys, but in fact there is evidence of this same desire manifest in collections of model soldiers, particularly those made of metal. So much so that in the nineteenth century it became a real industry, particularly in Germany, Switzerland and France, though still on a craft basis. Before then lead soldiers, 'table armies', were a luxury reserved for hereditary princes, soldiers of fortune and kings, who used these model soldiers to work out the phases of a battle or to reconstruct it in the comfort of their homes. No ordinary boy, therefore, could aspire to such playthings. They were prohibitively expensive: he had instead to console himself with paper soldiers glued on to rigid supports and carefully cut out.

The growing passion for collecting military miniatures (a phrase often preferred to their old title of model soldiers) has aroused a similar interest in their origins. Side by side with mass-produced modern pieces, which are now produced increasingly in plastic, the places of honour behind glass and on bookshelves are occupied by single items made of lead or plastic, carved or cast by first-class sculptors and miniaturists often endowed with real artistic talent. The figurine, which nowadays is almost always three-dimensional, with a standard size of 54 mm from head to foot (excluding headgear), has become, partly through the interest taken in it by architects and designers, a showpiece, a statuette to exhibit as one might do with Capodimonte and Meissen figures. The paper soldier, too, particularly if an eighteenth-century 'edition', has found a new and decorative popularity: on lampshades, wardrobes and wastepaper baskets.

It is an intriguing thought that while the ideal of peace is so earnestly pursued and modern-day militarism is frowned upon, the interest in military uniforms, particularly the most colourful ones, is flourishing everywhere, as can be seen from current fashion, minor arts and collecting. The number of people collecting and reworking military miniatures has never been greater than it is now: clubs and groups of enthusiasts, including young people, are springing up everywhere. Apart from mentioning the work of some collectors who have specialised in unusual subjects (prehistory, the Japanese Samurai, Ancient Egypt) this book will look particularly at the Napoleonic Empire – the period which produced perhaps the most popular variety of exotic uniforms – the American Civil War, and the First and Second World Wars. Uniforms, helmets, busbies, *aiguillettes*, sashes, *sabretaches*, bandoliers, armour, epaulets, shakos, sword-knots, scimitars, lances, pennants, ruffs, badges, swords and firearms of every kind – these are the details which fascinate the collectors of model soldiers today, people of all ages and from all walks of life.

# From historical figurines to tin soldiers

The history of military miniatures usually begins with Prince Emsah's guard. These are two groups of small wooden soldiers, painted and arranged in ranks of four and lines of eight men, each line fixed to a single stand so that the soldiers cannot be moved individually. They were found in the tomb of Prince Emsah, a hero – or at least a soldier of fortune – of the 12th Dynasty (about the year 2000 BC) during excavations at Assiut in Upper Egypt, and they are now in a showcase in the Cairo Museum (or at least they usually are: currently – in 1972 –

rumour has it that they have been put into storage). The two groups represent an Egyptian heavy infantry detachment armed with lance-javelins and swords slung point upwards – in exactly the opposite direction from medieval swords – and a platoon of light Numidian infantry, armed only with short spears. Their appearance is quite clearly that of soldiers as we understand the word today, but their purpose was completely different from those toys which came later. The Egyptian took with him to his tomb not only everyday implements and jewels for his use in the after-life but also miniature representations of those objects and beings which, animate or inanimate, it would have been impossible to bury with him. So at the side of the mummies can be found small boats, chariots and 'Scale HO' horses (as a modern collector would term them), statuettes representing workmen, servants, and so on. Thus Prince Emsah, because he was a warrior, would continue to be accompanied by his guard which was represented by these models.

The period between these Egyptian soldiers and those of relatively modern times, thousands of years later, produced few similar specimens, and this suggests a lack of interest among the ancients for 'table armies'. Exceptions of these blank centuries are the Roman legionary made of tin found at Magonza and attributed to the Imperial epoch, and two medieval knights also made of tin, one of which is in the museum at Cluny. But these exceptions are too few to allow us to presume any continuity of tradition. To complicate matters, at the end of the nineteenth century, when the passion for model soldiers was intense, a dishonest shopkeeper from the Rue de la Huchette in Paris took a hand. He made 'medieval' figurines and threw them at night into the Seine. Some days later he fished them out in the presence of witnesses who were ready to swear to their authenticity; the public rushed to see the 'antique' toys with the mud scarcely cleaned from them and for sale at 'antique' prices.

Historical model soldiers appeared only in the fifteenth century and became the playthings of hereditary princes.

We must not overlook the fact that by the late seventeenth century the art of war had become not only the prerogative of generals but also a kind of *salon* amusement: the works of the military theorist Vauban were studied and discussions, often with the ladies taking part, ranged over subjects which extended from the technicalities of a siege to the fundamental principles of fortification. These were the years of the big sieges, from La Rochelle to Turin – 'Big sieges please me best', Louis XIV once declared. So that the heir to the throne would be involved from early childhood with the duties which he would one day assume, he was given model soldiers to play with.

The most celebrated of these soldiers are the ones which Queen Marie de'Médicis had made for her son, the future Louis XIII. They were later inherited by Louis XIV who completed the collection with other models. Unfortunately for the student of today these were either models made of silver, which the King would send to the mint when he was short of funds, or hand-painted specimens of paper which have not survived the passing of the years. The tradition of warlike toys lasted for centuries: the heir of Napoleon III, the Prince Imperial (who did not succeed to the throne, being killed in the Zulu War of 1879) had a collection of uniforms, miniature armies and model soldiers. Nor did reigning monarchs stint themselves: in the San Martino Museum in Naples there is a showcase of Bourbon troops marching on parade with His Majesty King Ferdinand II at their head, together with hundreds of other cardboard model soldiers, all painted on both sides by the miniaturists Emanuele and Emilio Gin.

Up to now we have looked at a luxury denied to ordinary people, but by the end of the eighteenth century the difference of life-style was being changed by two important factors. First came the mixing of tin with other metals (lead, antimony, copper) to produce inexpensive alloys: this 'poor man's plate' allowed an increase in the number of metal plates, beakers, cutlery and even decorative objects as opposed to pottery and wood. At the

same time the growth of professional armies had already resulted in the standardisation of uniforms. These professional armies, important items of state expenditure, were also an expression of state power, and they soon began to interest the man in the street (and his children). It was therefore an entirely natural development for metalworkers and artists to produce and sell model soldiers made of tin and paper.

The paternity of the former is attributed by some to Johann Gottfried Hilpert, born in Coburg in 1732, who moved in 1750 to Nuremberg to practise his craft of metal foundry: he was followed by his sons and nephews and founded a dynasty which manufactured model soldiers for more than a century. The city where they lived became the production centre for new toys and even today gives its name to the flat two-dimensional figurines (the thickness is minimal) supported on a base, the moulding of which is individual to each maker. As always happens, their success brought other competitors into the market. Among the most famous were those of another great dynasty of craftsmen who made model soldiers, the Heinrichsens and an ex-workman of theirs, Johann Christian Allgeyer. It was these founders of families and their direct heirs who established the 'golden mean' of the Nuremberg model soldiers: height 30 mm for foot soldiers (from head to foot, so helmet, busby or shako were excluded) and 40 mm for mounted soldiers. The figurines were sold unpainted (as were the first models made in plastic a century and a half later) or painted, and always by weight. They were sold in wooden boxes (of 1 lb, $\frac{1}{2}$ lb, $\frac{1}{4}$ lb and $\frac{1}{8}$ lb) which were oval in shape and which contained from 20 to 150 soldiers of various armies. Since that time model soldiers have frequently been painted by enthusiasts in their homes.

The Nuremberg soldiers are greatly appreciated by children and also by certain collectors who buy them in their hundreds to reconstruct – although very approximately – battle scenes. The first eighteenth-century models, now so rare as to be unobtainable, reproduce with no great fidelity the uniforms and armies of the Seven Years War and Frederick the Great's Prussian army: then the Napoleonic adventure furnished a source – still being energetically worked today – of as many picturesque and attractive model soldiers as are required by popular demand. The golden age of the figurine was, however, from 1830 to 1890: to European uniforms were added colonial ones.

Although the Nuremberg soldiers seem attractive and fascinating, they do in fact, like their paper counterparts, have a certain remoteness from reality which renders them incomplete. Three-dimensional figurines (called in French *ronde-bosse*) were therefore a natural development. These *ronde-bosse* were very similar to statuettes in that they were solid and represented not only the human form but also the details of the uniform with greater accuracy. While the original solid model soldiers are not well documented (although the models owned by Louis XIV belonged to this type), the Parisian metalworker, Lucotte, is credited with having started, in about 1789, the production of 'little men' in French army uniform. For a long time, in France, Lucotte remained the patron of lead model soldiers (in fact a harder alloy was used, with antimony, very similar to the metal used in type founts). But around 1850 the craftsmen Cuberly, Blondel and Gerbeau provided competition for him, distinguishing their boxes of soldiers – stupendous confections in red and gold with a very elaborate label on the lid on which are depicted in an ever-increasing list the gold medals won at international exhibitions – with the trademark CBG. This still appears on today's labels – although the firm has been taken over by another competitor, Mignot – on special little boxes for collectors containing either four infantrymen or one mounted on horseback (almost always a portrait of Napoleon, Murat or another Napoleonic general). These famous model soldiers, packed in cellophane carrying the famous CBG trademark in gold, are often the first acquisition of a new collector or of people who want to enliven a glass case or shelf in their children's nursery with dolls that are less familiar than porcelain or ceramic ones.

There is also an international measure for *ronde-bosse*: 54 mm for foot soldiers, 70 mm for those on horseback (always remembering that headgear is excluded from these measurements). Naturally, and particularly when one moves away from animated models to stationary models, the measurements can change, but for purposes of comparison these are the standards of the collector.

About the year 1890, thanks to an English producer, William Britain, an important innovation was made which lowered the price considerably and allowed greatly increased and quicker production: the hollow *ronde-bosse*, which was obtained by a casting which left a very evident join on the model from the two halves of the mould. Aluminium alloys were also being tried out. The result of all this was the beginning of a decline in quality and boys were no longer attracted by model soldiers which they considered – rightly – to be ugly.

## Plastic and single models

In Europe, the years between 1918 and 1950 are the gloomiest in the history of model soldiers. During the First World War scarcity of metal ended regular production, and an absurd clause in the Treaty of Versailles prohibited Germany from making any toys which could be considered emblems of Prussian militarism. It practically spelt the end of the mass-produced Nuremberg figurines. Model soldiers were still available, certainly, but in the twenty-year period between the two world wars and in the period which immediately followed the second, children seemed to have forgotten model soldiers and turned towards other ideas: mechanical cars and toys were continually being improved; so were electric trains. Collecting itself seemed in the doldrums. Among the very rare exceptions was an exhibition of dioramas organised at the Castel Sant'Angelo in Rome in May 1937 by Johann Mauke, a German collector-manufacturer living in Naples who worked with Nuremberg-type figurines, choosing the most popular subject, the Napoleonic period. That

exhibition, to which the newspapers devoted ample space, was about the only existing evidence of Italian production – or rather Italian organised by a foreigner – of military miniatures. An article published in the *Nazione Militare* in that year stated that the jeweller Castellani owned a good collection of Allegeyer and Furth models.

In 1947 CBG of Paris started again to produce model soldiers made of tinplate and at prices which were still reasonable. In Germany, too, production was gradually restarted thanks to Aloys Ochel of Kiel and Babette Schweizer, and to Neckel of Stuttgart who had started production only in 1939. But all (or almost all) the Nuremberg models which came from these *ateliers* ended up in collectors' showcases, perhaps via antiquarians, who passed them off as nineteenth-century model soldiers. If the toy soldier was rediscovered during the 1950s, the credit for this must go to the English and to the new formula for making models in plastic.

For decades industry in general, but also the model soldier industry, had tried to substitute cheaper materials for tin and lead, which were both heavy and expensive. In 1936 the German Hausser (trademark 'Elastolin', still well-known today) remembered a raw material that at one time had been widely employed for making toys – papier-mâché. The results he obtained were passable, once the models had been coloured by hand, but lead was still superior. Shortly before the Second World War Hausser carried out research to see if new plastic materials which seemed very promising could be used, but an Allied air raid destroyed the pilot plant constructed even while Germany was at war. About 1947 Elastolin and other manufacturers started production again. But they found themselves challenged, as they had been on the battlefield, by the English.

Two names dominated the field in this post-war period. The first was Herald, or more precisely Herald Miniatures. The owner of this trademark, a Pole who went to England in 1908, M. Zang, became a toy manufacturer. After the Second World War Zang (who later amalgamated with

Britain) put out his first boxes of plastic Heralds containing subjects most of which are still being sold: British Guardsmen with their red tunics, the Household Cavalry, Scottish regiments, groups (including a metal cannon) of Confederate and Union soldiers, and, finally, toys which recaptured in full the interest of the boys: Cowboys and Indians. Success was assured. To military subjects were linked, even though they sold less well, non-military models (fox-hunting, factories, and zoos). Production rapidly increased: Britain relaunched their own products (which had been on the 'solid' market, as we have said, since 1893) and stepped up production with *Swoppets* (particularly medieval warriors) which could be taken apart and put together again. In 1956 Timpo and Crescent Toys appeared as manufacturers.

All these soldiers are of the *ronde-bosse* type of the standard 54-mm measurement: moulded – or rather pressed – in series. They are sold at very low prices, and are often rather crudely painted (not by the English, but by their continental competitors); but they are very pleasing (the 'movement' is almost always excellent) if they are well painted. Because of their cheapness these models are widely distributed: modelled in the United Kingdom, they were exported to Hong Kong where they were painted by local craftsmen, paid with the famous fistful of rice, and then returned to Europe. As a consequence there are Far Eastern competitors (in Hong Kong, of course, but also in the People's Republic of China) ready to copy uniforms of imperialist armies, to compete on the 'white' (unpainted) market. Because of this, for a long time collectors would not accept plastic.

About 1960 a French coffee-packing company helped to break down this barrier. It included unpainted French model soldiers made of Starlux plastic in its packets and offered money prizes for the best-painted models. The competition was a success: collectors realised that if finished properly they could – even if made of polyethylene or similar material – be beautiful. So plastic began to be accepted by collectors and by 'sculptors' of single pieces.

It was an important and exciting event when Elastolin

started producing again (specialising in pikemen, mercenaries and siege engines). In France Segom also forged ahead, extending its range of subjects from the period of Louis XIV to the Second Empire, and concentrating more on quality productions. Mauke (whom we have already mentioned), Charles-Félix Keller, a Swiss living in Paris, and Maître Philippot, the Paris notary, and for years President of the Collectors' Society, all set up armies of models. These were almost exclusively Nuremberg, of thirty to forty thousand men, used to reconstruct, with almost the same number of troops as their originals, entire episodes from the battles of Leipzig, Wagram or Waterloo. (A very noteworthy collection in Italy, at the beginning of the 1960s, was that of Colonel Nicolò Maraini in Rome, who reported that he had built up a collection of about 60,000 pieces.)

This new wave of collecting went in for quality rather than quantity: some tens of pieces (they rarely reached the hundred mark), very beautiful, singly made, painted with care so that they resembled statuettes rather than model soldiers. And as minor sculpture they were adopted (as we have already remarked) by architects and interior designers to add an additional something to houses, libraries and nurseries. So for some years yet one will be able to see groups of *ronde-bosse* figures in Napoleonic uniforms, or colour parties of the Royal Deux-Ponts or Royal Italien in homes whose owners have no interest whatsoever in military collecting.

For some years, the small printed catalogue from Norman Newton in London has listed pieces made singly by two English specialists. Richard Courtenay was one of the pioneers (he started to manufacture model soldiers – particularly 'portraits' of medieval knights, from the Black Prince to Henry V – in 1928). The second is the excellent Charles Stadden, who started to work only in 1951 but who quickly became famous for his *atelier* models, particularly – and this is where he differed from the others – with his Indian cavalry of the late nineteenth century. The Stadden catalogue had an impressive price list: a single figurine cost more than £2 ($5), a couple

(a famous one is an officer of the 7th Bengal Lancers shaking hands with an officer from Skinner's Horse) around £5 ($12·50) Another English craftsman-producer is Russell Gammage (trademark Rose Models), who supplies not only complete model soldiers but also unpainted pieces ready for modification by the specialists we shall discuss later. All these figurines are to the standard 54-mm measurement.

In France one of the most famous names left among those craftsmen with a workshop capable of supplying some hundreds of examples is Madame Fernande Métayer. 'I was widowed during the war', she says. 'I was not trained for anything: I was a typical example of a well-brought-up young lady who played the piano, painted in watercolours and embroidered. It was my painting which hinted at a possible solution for me: model soldiers. I started to do some research and to design them and I found a sculptor who could complete my designs for me. I painted them. I was lucky. My 'little men' travel all over Europe, to America, particularly to the museums.' Madame, who enjoys the collaboration of one of the best-known designers of figurines, Lucien Rousselot (he is the maker of the Nuremberg models reproduced in this book), also sells complete dioramas. An important use for model soldiers which we shall see when we come to talk about dioramas is for reconstructing – as faithfully as possible – scenes from the life of their period.

Side by side with the very small industries, and much more numerous, are isolated craftsmen capable of producing pieces for serious collectors. These makers found themselves able to work entirely on their own and to make a few – very few – miniatures which were, understandably, more beautiful and more expensive than those made in the ateliers where as many as a dozen people work. This 'trade' started in France around 1941 – the year of Fernande Métayer – during the German Occupation. At first it was the goldsmiths, unemployed because there were no precious metals, who started the work, using the minute oxyhydrogen blowlamps which were normally used for brooches, bracelets and necklaces.

These 'masters' went to work to make statuettes copied from 'commercial' model soldiers. These were well made and found buyers easily. At the end of the war some of these artisans had become specialists, the market had suddenly expanded, not least through the merits of the designers of whom we have spoken, and they maintained their output. Today the beautiful, individually made figurines of Mademoiselle Josiane Desfontaines, for example, are extremely rare and are much sought after by collectors.

Several small organisations produce figures with individual character. There is Edward Surén, whose firm 'Willie Figures' is in London's Lower Sloane Street. He is noted for the action which he puts into his wide range of figures. Another successful British manufacturer is Hinton Hunt. Marcus Hinton's figures have a rugged charm that is all their own.

In fact, collecting has never contented itself purely and simply with model soldiers of the past, which are pleasing but somewhat removed from everyday life. Complete and accurate documentation is a must. There have always been enthusiasts who collect not model soldiers but documents on military history, uniform regulations, treatises on strategy and the art of fortification, and manuals precise to the point of pedantry in which are detailed the colours and characteristics of headgear, tunics, braiding, chevrons, wristbands, edgings, epaulets and badges of rank. 'Uniformology' has become a new science. Specialist painters follow in the footsteps of the Italian artists of the seventeenth century, like Quinto Cenni, who documented the Italian Army of Umberto I; in France there are 'masters of battle' like Edouard Détaille (who, when he paints military pictures, likes to put on a military tunic and *képi*), De Neuville and Morot. Their work has appeared in libraries and clubs: there are sheets from *Le Plumet*, created by Rousselot (more than a hundred, almost all devoted to the Napoleonic Empire), and, in even greater numbers, those of Eugène Leliepvre.

In Great Britain the military journal *Tradition* has printed others. Thirty years after the first printing the

German publisher Kleitmann reprinted sheets from *Heer Und Tradition*. The Americans, too, have brought out studies and publications devoted to their own wars. Usually a picture will illustrate not only the complete uniform but also details from it, particularly embroidery, edging, rank badges and frogging. There are books – in English – which deal only with buttons and medals.

The man who makes model soldiers must know all this: generally he does and he willingly keeps up to date. In Italy, for instance, the 1971 Proceedings of the Academy of San Marciano in Turin exemplify what is happening in many countries. This is a high-powered association of collectors and students of antique arms, military history and 'standardology' (the study of flags, standards and pennants, a subject connected, particularly for figures depicting standard bearers, with model soldiers).

The Luciano Antonini company in Rome produces only one series: pure lead, solid, to the usual 54-mm size. Although these are not animated models, the Antonini models still have the ingenuous – one might almost say primitive – appeal of certain nineteenth-century model soldiers closer to toys than to miniature sculpture. Antonini is one of the very few specialists in Italian uniforms of the late nineteenth century, of the two world wars and of the present day. Recently he concluded an agreement with one of the best Italian makers of single pieces, Dr Pranzetti of Sassari, to translate his models into lead and manufacture them in series. (Usually Pranzetti works in wood: his cavalry figurines can be seen in the colour plates of the Artesi collection.)

Ernesto Chiappa of Turin produces single pieces, usually soldiers of the eighteenth-century Piedmontese armies, in wood and other materials (cloth, metal and leather) with great accuracy. At Altare near Savona are the two Bormiolis, Alfio the father and Amanzio the son; they also make lead figures, single models, as usual to the 54-mm measure. Although on a small scale, Genoa is becoming a centre of production with four craftsmen working in the field of individual pieces: Gian Roberto Parisini, Tuscan by birth, who started casting in metal

after experimenting with cardboard and wax models; Giannetto Bruzzone, a teacher of design and the history of art, who modifies plastic figurines finished with threads of iron, lead, wood, cardboard and clay; and Andrea Oneto and Giovanni Rocchiero who are also making *ronde-bosse*.

In Milan there are some young people making unusual model soldiers in lead or plastic: among these are the architect Maurizio Boverio, a specialist in plastics, and Gianni Tura who specialises in a little-known subject: Japanese Samurai.

There are still three sectors which should be noted. First plastic kits, production of which is dominated by the French company Historex and their English rival, Airfix. These provide the complete parts of soldiers and their equipment, sold in boxes or envelopes which the collector (or in this case the modeller) can construct for himself, gluing the different pieces together and painting them with specially manufactured paints. Historex produces for the most part soldiers of the First Empire (at least half military collecting is absorbed by that period, the most popular because of the rich uniforms) sold in envelopes. Among die-hard collectors these figurines are regarded with a certain scepticism, but undoubtedly they represent a form of modelling which is growing in popularity.

Secondly, among the new groups is that of very small model soldiers (HO scale 1:86, between 18 and 20 mm). This field is led by Airfix, which also makes kit models of ships, aeroplanes, armoured vehicles and motor cars to be put together at home. Sold in boxes of 48 pieces (a few less if there are also horses and cannon) in plastic, of uniform colour, these 'minis' appeared initially to be almost entirely plastic accessories for armoured vehicles, airfields, railways. Gradually it was seen that it was possible, by using very fine paint brushes and a lot of patience, to paint American marines and Japanese infantry so as to have acceptable figurines – a good size for a modern War Game. Since then Airfix has increased its range of models (Egyptians, Roman legionaries,

Russian armies and many more) and enthusiasts value them highly. Maurizio Boverio for example has reconstructed the siege of Dien Bien Phu with them and has also assembled a scene of the Black Watch at Waterloo using these models.

Finally a phenomenon which burst upon the world unexpectedly in 1965 and has had enormous, if weakening, repercussions in the course of a few years: Action Man.

Action Man is a doll about one foot high made of plastic, articulated, and with an enormous number of uniforms, accessories, weapons and instruments of all kinds. In practice, babies and children who are given Action Man treat him as a doll, undressing and dressing him in the uniforms of different armies – from the Russian to the Nazi – or underwater or astronaut gear or whatever.

The success of Action Man – the only positive attraction for a collector being the invitation to a greater study of uniforms – led to the introduction of other similar dolls: Major Matt Mason, space hero; Captain Action (who, thanks to changes of costume, can be transformed into Batman, Flash Gordon and others) and heroes of the Wild West. Different in that they cannot be dressed up, but similar to Action Man, are Airfix kits (this term in itself signifies something to be assembled) of Napoleon, Cromwell, Richard Coeur de Lion and others which can be assembled in the home. These models have never enjoyed the popularity of the model ships and aeroplanes, although their detail is good. Meanwhile, in 1972, Action Man, the military doll, soldiers on. . . .

# Paper soldiers

It is impossible to establish exactly the date of the first true paper model soldier, as distinct from the popular print representing a king or prince in the uniform of a hussar or grenadier, used purely for decoration. The distinction between decorative prints and the model toy soldier comes when one thinks of cut-outs: sticking the

sheet on to cardboard and making scissor cut-outs with which one can play. According to historiographers of model soldiers the discovery occurred in 1744 in Strasbourg, thanks to the printer Seyfried. It was he who, noting the interest aroused in the city by the arrival of many troops escorting Louis XV on an official visit, thought of making souvenir sheets with pictures of these soldiers. The idea pleased him, the model soldiers sold, and Seyfried quickly found himself challenged by rivals such as Pietro Francesco Isnard, cavalry officer, poet and writer, who printed five sheets of uniforms between 1776 and 1779, and Gian Federico Striedbeck, who called himself a 'manufacturer of painted troops'. It was the period in which Strasbourg could consider itself the capital of paper model soldiers: a supremacy which found its greatest expression during the Second Empire in the activities of Rodolfo Silbermann, whose output reached 130,000 sheets a year.

Others, however, were not idle. At Epinal in the Vosges, the Pellerin Brothers and particularly Jean Charles (1756–1836) did not restrict themselves during the Napoleonic period to printing and selling their *Images d'Epinal* (saints, proverbs, battles of the Empire): they extended their interest to uniforms. Initially the sheets they printed depicted only four or five models each: then came two, three, four and more lines of soldiers which, of course, reduced the size of the models. Printing was by xylography (wood blocks). At Epinal in the storehouses of the Pellerin Company there still exist the hand-cut wooden *planches* (today zinc plates are used). Colouring was done by hand with 'masks' of card cut-out over which the paintbrush dipped in aniline colours was passed.

In Italy – strangely, 'official histories' of model soldiers seem to ignore it – it was the Remondinis of Bassano del Grappa who launched the Strasbourg sheets. This famous printing family has disappeared today but, particularly in the mid eighteenth century under the guidance of Giuseppe Remondini, it was a power in the field of popular publishing: twelve printing presses, four active

papermakers, two hundred families (then fathers and sons all followed the same trade) at work both in the shop and at home, hand-colouring prints of all kinds, from saints to playing cards, from parade cards to military costumes. Remondini pictures were sold everywhere, so much so that sacred pictures with prayers in Spanish, German and even Cyrillic characters (for the Eastern Church) were printed at Bassano. Naturally there was no shortage of model soldiers. Recently a printer from Bassano, Zillio, has reprinted, by photolitho, some sheets of dragoons, foot soldiers, musicians, all in two lines, simply designed – the uniforms for the most part invented but pleasing nevertheless. In 1859 the Remondini printing works closed, having been in difficulties for some time. For more than 20 years no Italian military figurines appeared.

But in Milan in 1878 production started again with Lebrun and Boldetti lithography and, a few years later, with other Milanese lithographers: Vedova Vertua, Mercenaro and Macchi, Aristide Giore, De Castiglione. Between 1895 and 1910 production increased because the manufacturers had excellent models to rely on, those of the painter Quinto Cenni whom we have already mentioned. The First World War brought an increase in printings (never before, perhaps, had Italian children played so much with model soldiers) of other models, copies from coloured plates by Achille Beltrame in the *Domenica del Corriere*. It was the period of the Stella and Aquila trademarks – not yet completely forgotten by present-day grandparents. The decline began in the 1930s: mediocre production (Carroccio and Cartoccino editions were above the average) and modest attempts to interest children with new subjects (Soviet troops, armoured vehicles, Cowboys and Indians).

Since 1950 there has been practically nothing new in this field except for sheets of cardboard printed on both sides and devoted to a few famous regiments (Europa Editions). Pellerin reproduced their soldiers nearly life-size (about five feet tall) for this express purpose. Subjects easily obtainable are the zouaves of the Second Empire,

the canteen girl, and the Prince Imperial in grenadier uniform. In antique shops it is possible to find sheets of model soldiers printed in Spain and Germany at the end of the nineteenth century, but they are expensive.

## Showcases and dioramas

The greatest problem for those who collect model soldiers is how to set them out. The easiest solution is to leave them in their own boxes or in special display cases, and to take them out to look at as one likes. With this in mind – and as some colour plates in this book show – there are manufacturers who have packaged their models, particularly animated ones, in boxes with coloured pictures at the bottom and the models so arranged as to make a scene. But if money and space – the two greatest obstacles for a collector – allow, the collector prefers dioramas.

The most important Italian collection, which is so vast that it could be considered to be a museum on its own, is at Ponte di Brenta near Padua and belongs to the heirs of Commendatore Testi who created it some years ago, devoting one entire floor of his villa to his collection. Dioramas, using model soldiers of all kinds, are arranged in special showcases. The *ronde-bosse* alone total more than 20,000 and there are many Antonini models from Rome, especially in scenes from Italian history. Among the most interesting dioramas: a squadron of Genoese Cavalry in eighteenth-century uniform, the Battle of the Volturno (with portrait figures of Garibaldi, Bixio, Cosenz and others); a parade of Royal Piedmont Cavalry framed in a march-past with Umberto I taking the salute; and another review depicting Wilhelm II in Berlin in front of the Brandenburg Gate. Naturally for the average collector it is easier to make dioramas on a smaller scale (the Testi dioramas each occupy a frontage of about three to five feet) and with fewer models. One basic point: if the scene is historical the diorama itself ought also to include a faithful portrayal of the countryside at that time. Here further research is needed

13

and analysis of prints, designs, historical pictures (for centuries before Daguerre – or Brady, the photographer-reporter of the American Civil War – armies very often had in their train their own painter-documentarist), notebooks and photograph albums must be made. Model railway accessories which are offered for sale include trees, bushes, rocks, embankments and ruined castles, and are a great help in the construction of these externals. And it is the availability of these pieces modelled to the HO scale which is the reason for the increasing use of very small model plastic soldiers.

There are other famous dioramas on show. Since 1948, there has been at Compiègne a museum devoted to military miniatures which currently houses a collection of about 90,000 models. Among the dioramas there is the Battle of Waterloo, approximately 270 square feet with about 12,000 Nuremberg model soldiers. Also to be found is a military review at Betheny in 1910 with 12,000 ronde-bosse, in French uniform, and (the work of Michel Ballada, a present-day master) a group representing the funeral of Napoleon (the so-called 'return of the ashes') which took place in Paris when the British returned Napoleon's remains from St Helena to France in 1840.

One of the most famous dioramas (from the number of models displayed) used to be on show at the Royal United Services Institution's Museum in London until its closure in 1962. It was started in 1816 by Captain Siborne, who dedicated years of work to it. In all he had around 180,000 models made, barely 12 mm high, and, as Marcel Baldet has written, decidedly ugly. This model now belongs to the National Army Museum, but it is at present in store. Siborne made a smaller diorama with larger and very attractive figures, which shows the fighting around La Haye Sainte at Waterloo. It is kept for display at Dover Castle. In its prime, the Royal United Services Institution's Museum exhibited 15 dioramas, made about 1935 for the collector Otto Gottstein and showing various scenes from English history.

We have wandered somewhat from the discussion of real collecting to consider how historical figurines enable museums to reconstruct with great vividness scenes from past life in a way not possible with drawings or paintings. Most of the collections devoted to military history or costume use dioramas. These collections include a famous one at Cologne; the Carnavalet Museum and the *Musée de l'Armée* in Paris; museums at West Point, at Albany (where there are scenes showing the discovery of America), at Leipzig, and so on. Other temporary dioramas can be prepared for exhibitions and shows: for an exhibition at Leipzig in 1930 around 150 were collected.

Dioramas often require types of figurine which are not much in demand as toys: non-military subjects. Almost all the manufacturers produce these models (which can be most attractive – CBG models can be seen in the colour plates). Britain offers, in plastic, a factory, a zoo, and a fox hunt. Among those at present on the market there are some 'reprints' of German models. These include the circus figures probably made by Heinrichsen at the end of the nineteenth century. Other civilian figurines, sold at high prices by Kober of Vienna, represent ladies, officials, and well-brought up children of the *Felix Austria* of Franz Josef.

# The war game

By far the most entertaining use of model soldiers is in the war game (it used to be called by its German title *Kriegspiel*). This is played across the wide surface area of a simulated, table-top battlefield, model soldiers, guns and vehicles being moved like pieces according to detailed rules, under the control of an umpire. These games can in theory be played with pins with coloured heads, each representing a company, a squadron, or armoured vehicles; but models are preferred since they are more interesting. Each move involves a lot of careful re-positioning, and the bigger the table the harder this is.

Although some games have an imaginary setting, the normal war game begins with the troops set out as they were on the eve of battle: at dawn on 18 June 1815 at

Waterloo, or on 6 June 1944 at the beginning of the 'longest day' along the Normandy beaches. The information on such dispositions will have been culled from orders of battle, reports and war plans published in history books. Then each combatant (sometimes as many as four for each opposing side) 'opens fire', moving the troops in which he is interested on the basis of tables. These can be extremely complicated, especially when they deal with contemporary armies and have to establish speed of movement, range of weapons, time for revictualling, and efficacy of attack. For example, an average armoured car proceeds $2\frac{1}{4}$ inches if on its own, 2 inches if in a column, and after 100 moves must be refuelled to be able to move in the correct relationship with other vehicles advancing according to other moves.

The effect of each move, especially the number of enemy casualties it causes – the effect of a field gun's shot, for instance – is gauged by a throw of the dice. The damage done to the enemy – whether by solid shot or explosive shell – is assessed by the number shown by the dice. The same applies to all arms – infantry, cavalry, armour, and even naval warships, which have war games of their own.

At one time Nuremburg model soldiers were used 'in battle' with a ratio of one to five, ten, thirty, or whatever; today, with the smaller plastic figures available, the ratio has been reduced to one to three: 30 figures represent a company of 90 men; six toy armoured vehicles represent 18 'live' ones. Sectors of artillery fire are established with triangular frames made of wire; the dice decide which areas inside the triangle are the most 'deadly'.

The war game and the desire to exchange, sell, or simply to let one's models be seen has given rise to many collectors' clubs. These are found all over the world. One of the oldest is *La Société des Collectionneurs de Figurines Historiques* of Paris, founded in 1930, which amalgamated in 1970 with the group of uniformology enthusiasts in *La Sabretache* (a total of around 150 members). In America, Austria, Belgium, Great Britain and Australia there are very active associations which publish bulletins, proceedings or journals (the British *Tradition*, devoted to uniformology and model soldiers, being almost a luxury production). In Italy enthusiasts can join the *Unione Nazionale Collezionisti d' Italia* with its head office in Rome, at Torre dei Conti in the Via dell'Impero, where there is also a small museum of model soldiers.

At one time, as in Pierre Benoit's novel *Axelle*, collectors of model soldiers were described as frustrated warmongers, seeking to transform the theory of the war game into practice, to assume command of real battalions after arranging their models carefully in boxes or in a showcase. The present-day collector, however, is a uniform enthusiast and a student of military history, who has firmly decided to go no further than displaying and admiring his models or reconstructing completely inoffensive armies with dioramas or table-top war games. There are those who think that the more they study war the less it is likely to happen. Perhaps it is better to work out one's aggression on the table-top rather than the battlefield. Nuclear warfare, after all, lacks the panache of Austerlitz and Jena. And with a collection of model soldiers, Everyman becomes his own Napoleon!

1  2

**1-2** The so-called 'model soldiers' of Prince Emsah, a soldier of fortune in the 12th Egyptian Dynasty, found during excavations at Assiut in Upper Egypt and now in the Cairo Museum. These are not in fact toys but funeral grave-goods, considered as essential for the after-life of a great warrior. They represent a detachment of Numidian light infantry armed with short lances, and an equally strong detachment of Egyptian heavy infantry with lances and shields. Archaeological evidence such as this shows how for centuries military figurines served as decorative objects or votive offerings rather than as toys or pawns for the manoeuvres of miniature armies. Certainly they were not created for the character formation of a future warrior-king. Towards the end of the fifteenth century 'tournament warriors', clearly intended as playthings, began to appear. These took the form of puppet knights. And by the mid seventeenth century model soldiers suitable for the education of princes had appeared at court. The most famous were the silver model soldiers made in France during the first half of the seventeenth century; a few of these were given by Queen Marie de' Médicis to the nine-year-old King Louis XIII, who in turn gave them to his son. These models later enriched the collection of the Dauphin (memoirs of the period speak of 'a large number of boxes'), for whom Vauban, the great military architect, made special *'constructions'* on which the precious models could be made to move. They were *too* precious, however: it seems that the *Roi Soleil* had them melted down for money. Napoleon also took pains to see that his son, the King of Rome, had his army of model soldiers. In 1812 the goldsmith Claude Odiot modelled a company of 117 model soldiers of the 22nd Light Regiment. These models, their uniforms suitably converted, followed the King of Rome to Vienna for his upbringing as an Austrian prince after Napoleon's downfall. Inherited by Napoleon III, they were given by the Empress Eugénie to the Souberain de Pierres family who still have them. Cardboard model soldiers were also very popular at court: they were individually hand-painted and were made of less expensive material. But they were no less expensive: Louis XIV's paper army of 20 cavalry squadrons and 10 infantry battalions cost, as long ago as the eighteenth century, over 32,000 Old Francs.

3

4

5

**3-4** A Royal Maundy Thursday procession, with King Ferdinand II of Naples, his Queen, the General Staff and the Diplomatic Corps, on painted paper. The most important Italian collection of painted paper model soldiers is in the San Martino Museum in Naples. It consists of 2,260 figures about 70 mm high, painted on both sides. These represent the military uniforms of the Kingdom of Naples, portraits of lords, ladies and dignitaries of the Bourbon court, and detachments of the Italian army which were to be found in the province of Campania between 1860 and 1870. The collection represents the work of two painters: Emanuele Gin, a French citizen born in Naples in 1817, and his son, Filippo Emilio, born in 1845. Emanuele was a landscape painter who later in

life became French Consul at Hamburg and Lübeck. He began to paint figurines for the court of Naples, and for the Count of Trapani in particular. This Maundy Thursday procession was his work. The detail worked into every figure is impressive.

**5-6** The work of Filippo Gin – Piedmontese infantry and light cavalry, also from the San Martino Museum. The entire collection was acquired by the Museum in 1923. There are other excellent collections of individually-painted paper model soldiers in the *Musée de l'Armée* in Paris and in the Army Museum in Madrid.

6

7

**7-8-9** Nuremberg 'flats' – knights and ensigns of the Teutonic Order, German hussars of 1830 and Bavarian infantry of 1880. Nuremberg was the birthplace of model tin soldiers as popular toys. The soldiers in these plates are modern castings from original moulds, which were of Thuringian slate, one for each side of the model. These moulds produced figures which were only a few millimetres thick and which had barely discernible relief markings on both sides. A few German museums still have these grey 'primitives' – it was only later that the figures began to be painted and transformed by highlighting the colour details of tunics, frogging, and facings on the uniforms of soldiers of different regiments. Foreign soldiers as well as German were represented. Johann Gottfried Hilpert has been described as 'the father of tin soldiers'. He started to transform all this into an ordered business, lining up production (which had been on the increase in Nuremberg since about 1730) with a distribution network and extensive sale abroad. Hilpert was born at Coburg in 1732 but moved to Nuremberg in 1750, where he was obliged to work for seven years as an apprentice tinsmith before he could obtain permission to work on his own, specialising in model soldiers. These models are from the Testi Collection at Ponte di Brenta, near Padua.

8

9

**10-11** Variations on a theme: naval subjects depicted in the medium of the Nuremberg 'flat' figure. They show an ironclad passing a coastal fort and lighthouse, and a German battleship. Both figures are from the Testi Collection. Several makers maintained the tradition set by Hilpert in Nuremberg. Johann Ludwig Stahl took over his firm and continued production. Then there were makers such as J. W. Gottschalk (1768–1843) and one of his pupils, Rudolf Weherli (1801–1876). Father-and-son tradition was kept up by the Reich, Ammon, and Schweizer families. And finally there came the 'codifier' of the Nuremberg style, Ernst Heinrichsen (1806–1888). He ranked with the very best makers during the 'golden age' of the Nuremberg 'flats', which began about 1830 and ended with large-scale production at the end of the century. His figures were not only more sophisticated in detail: he set a standard scale for their size. Until Heinrichsen's time there had been no standard measure and this type of figure had varied considerably in height. But in 1848, by agreement with other makers, Heinrichsen established the basic measurement of 30 mm for a foot soldier (excluding headgear) and 40 mm for figures on horseback. This measurement was destined to conquer the whole world market for this type of figure.

10

11

**12-13** Medieval knights in the service of the Duke of Burgunday, and Potsdam 'Giant Grenadiers' of the Prussian army of the eighteenth century. The difference between the unpainted and the completely painted 'flat' is clearly shown. These figures are by Aloys Ochel, photographed by Philip Stearns. Again, these are modern figures made from eighteenth-century moulds. The 30-mm Nuremberg figure, once accepted, became collected and copied everywhere. The French, who pioneered the three-dimensional 'round' model soldier, adopted the style of the Nuremberg soldier. In the second half of the nineteenth century the German model soldiers were sold by weight in oval wooden boxes similar to cheese or ointment boxes, including decorative elements like trees, trench parapets, etc. Value for money worked out approximately at 150 model foot soldiers per lb., and about half that number if they were mounted on horseback or supplied with cannon. Presentation for the customer was gradually improved until very attractive red and gold (and occasionally blue) boxes appeared, with their contents laid out on a sheet of white cardboard with the base supports of each model fitting into slots in the card, holding the model securely.

**14** Even the French, who were leading pioneers of the solid figurine, adopted the style of the Nuremberg 'flat'. These models are by Mignot of Paris. They show a bugler of Carabiniers and two *Grenadiers à Cheval* of Napoleon's Grand Army (Alberini Collection).

**15-16** Two box-showcases by CBG Mignot, offering the meeting between Joan of Arc and the Dauphin and including a detachment of knights facing halberdiers and crossbow-men; and scenes from Napoleon's invasion of Egypt.

13
14

15

16

19

**17-18** German Uhlans and Russian infantry, by Babette Schweizer. These figures reflect the increasing pursuit of detail which would in time produce model soldiers which were historical documents, not toys. In the second half of the nineteenth century the Allgeyer and Schweizer families were producing these 'mezzo-tondo' soldiers: basically the familiar Nuremberg 'flat', but thicker and moulded with much higher relief. The Schweizer dynasty of model soldier manufacturers was founded by Adam Schweizer in 1796, and has continued to this day. Babette Schweizer made the soldiers in these plates from moulds which have been kept in the family. Today the production of Nuremberg 'flats' is far less widely practised than that of 'round' figures, which are much more popular with collectors. Beside Babette Schweizer and CBG

Mignot there is also Aloys Ochel of Kiel, who began making model soldiers in 1945. He has produced an enormous range of 'flats', from the Romans to the American Civil War (see plates 12–13).

**19** An interesting group of figures, also made from a Schweizer mould. It shows how far Franco-German bitterness was taken after Prussia's defeat of France in 1871: an arrogant Prussian soldier pushes a cringing French infantryman in front of a Prussian general. Only rarely are model soldiers given jingoistic poses like this nowadays, and when this does happen an element of humour is often present as an antidote. Military modellers are concerned with other things than nationalistic spite.

**20** Civilian figures have always interested modellers, and deserve a mention here. Apart from the useful role they play in creating realistic non-military scenes – good civilian figures have always been in great demand by railway modellers, for example – they have also attracted much attention from military modellers of the first degree. Plate 20 shows a diorama containing figures by Josef Kober of Vienna. Here the very ingenuousness of the figures adds to the *fin de siècle* charm and elegance of this scene in a Viennese park, complete with well brought-up children, ladies dressed in the peak of fashion, and dashing officers in their walking-out uniforms gallantly escorting their ladies. These are '*mezzo-tondo*' – semi-round – figures, marking the half-way stage in the evolution of the fully-round miniature figure.

**21-22** These two elaborate dioramas are also technically 'civilian' scenes, but the figures used in them are far more advanced. They were made by Mademoiselle Josiane Desfontaines, a brilliant artist in the field of military miniatures, for the collection of Brigadier Peter Young. The subject is 'scenes in the life of Casanova'. Special photography by Philip Stearns highlights the amazing degree of detail which can be worked into a miniature figure by a first-class maker.

21

22

**23-24** The Imperial Austrian Army did not have a very successful record in the nineteenth century, with gory defeats by the French at Solferino in 1859 and by the Prussians at Königgrätz in 1866. But it was as colourful as any of its contemporaries, and these figures by Kober of Vienna show a real if somewhat ingenuous pride in the appearance of the Austrian army on the eve of the First World War. Kober's group 'The Emperor on Manoeuvres' contains 26 lead *mezzo-tondo* figures, all 30 mm high. In the diorama – reproduced from photographs by Bevilacqua – the Emperor, mounted on his white horse, scans the horizon through his binoculars, surrounded by the officers of his staff, his bodyguard, even by horse-holders. Models like this inspired the birth of the great collections, assembled by people faithful to the Heinrichsen style who were able to buy different boxes of infantry and cavalry by the lb. to set out imposing armies. Modern enthusiasts prepare to concentrate on a few beautiful models rather than to go in for thousands of comparatively featureless ones, but several of the big collections still survive.

They include that of M Philippot, President of the Parisian *La Sabretache*, who has around forty thousand pieces; and, at Ponte di Brenta in Italy, the exceptional collection of the late Luigi Testi, now the property of his two sons.

**25** This illustrates the startling difference of the *ronde-bosse*. The figures in this small diorama of a 1917 encounter 'somewhere in France' are from the excellent Stadden range of completely 'round' and finely detailed miniature figures. The diorama itself, from Norman Newton Ltd., Piccadilly, represents a meeting between the pilot of a German Fokker Dr-1 Triplane and curious German cavalrymen. The fully 'round' model soldier was the logical development of the Nuremberg 'flats' and later 'semi-round' figures. Pioneered by Mignot in France and William Britain in England, these 'round' figures (or *ronde-bosse*, as they are known in France) soon won the interest of collectors. As with the Nuremberg 'flats', a standard measure was adopted for the *ronde-bosse*: 54 mm.

26 Another nostalgic group by Kober of Vienna: the car in which the Archduke Franz Ferdinand of Austria and his wife were shot dead in Sarajevo, 1914 – the incident which triggered off the First World War. The figures in this group are fixed in pairs to lead bars placed in the seats. They are 'round' figures, slightly flattened, and 30 mm high.

27 Portrait figure by Kober: His Imperial Majesty Franz Josef of Austria-Hungary, wearing the uniform of Generalissimo of the Empire. Franz Josef (born in 1830, and monarch from 1848 to 1916) had become a deeply respected figure by his death. Even today he frequently appears on tourist souvenirs – postcards, ashtrays, leatherwork, etc. In the Kober catalogue there are many representations of Franz Josef in various uniforms.

28 Kober 'semi-round' figures show men of the Austrian army of 1910 in battle order. These gunners are 30 mm high. Like Franz Ferdinand and the Emperor Franz Josef in the previous plates, these figures are slightly flattened. The field gun, however, is completely three-dimensional, and its wheels revolve.

29 A trooper of the Almanza Lancers – a crack regiment of Spanish cavalry – in the uniform of about 1850. This is a fully 'round' figure by Chauve (Alberini Collection). It measures 30 mm, the same measure as a Nuremberg 'flat'. Although this particular model does not lend itself particularly well to photographic enlargement, it has an attractive pose and is a good example of the work of one of the most prominent Spanish military modellers, who has produced several impressive models.

30 An impressive French *poilu* of the time of the Battle of Verdun in 1916, by the French modeller Marcel Baldet. It was photographed by Philip Stearns, to whose collection it belongs.

29  30

# ARTILLERIE avec Canons

IMAGERIE PELLERIN IMAGERIE D'ÉPINAL. N° 170

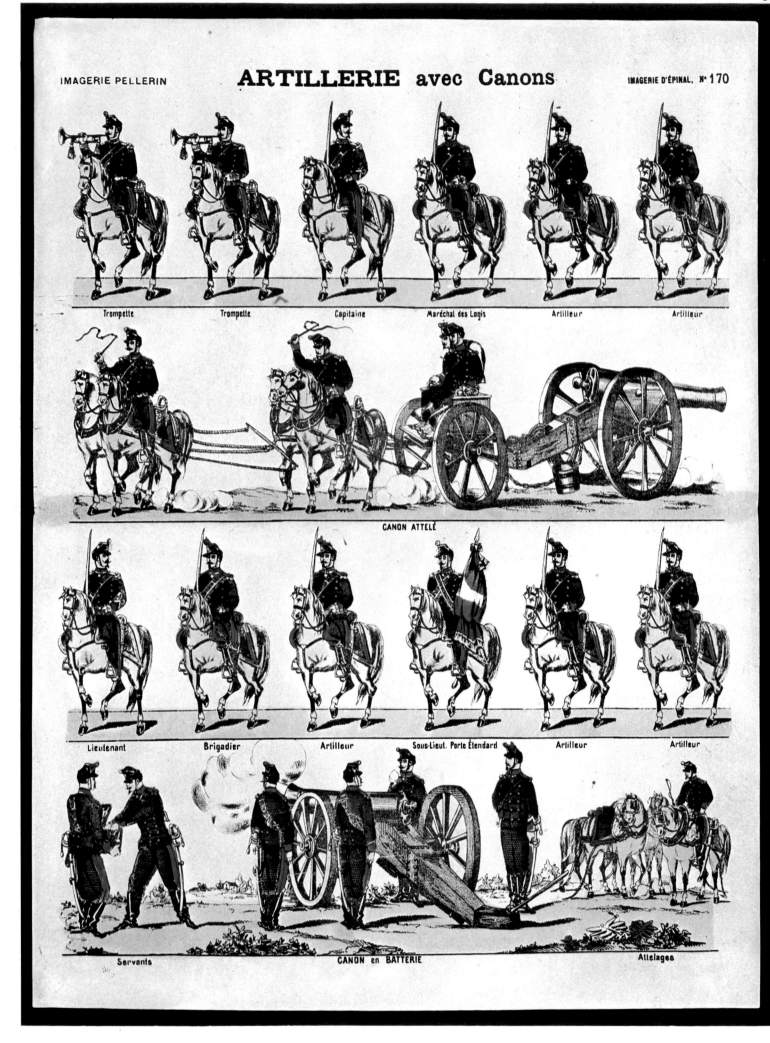

Trompette    Trompette    Capitaine    Maréchal des Logis    Artilleur    Artilleur

CANON ATTELÉ

Lieutenant    Brigadier    Artilleur    Sous-Lieut. Porte Étendard    Artilleur    Artilleur

Servants    CANON en BATTERIE    Attelages

**31-35** Colourful prints by the Imagerie Pellerin of Epinal. The popularity of these sheets dates back to the days of the Napoleonic Empire. Originally printed as hand-coloured wood engravings, modern day Pellerin prints use photolitho printing. But the overall result is much the same: striking and decorative presentment of military uniforms, which can be displayed either uncut or pasted on to card and carefully cut out.

**31** Cavalry and artillery of the French Second Empire.

**32** Italian cavalrymen.

**33** Prussian Uhlan buglers.

**34** Band of French cuirassier regiment.

**35** Officer and men of Italian Bersaglieri.

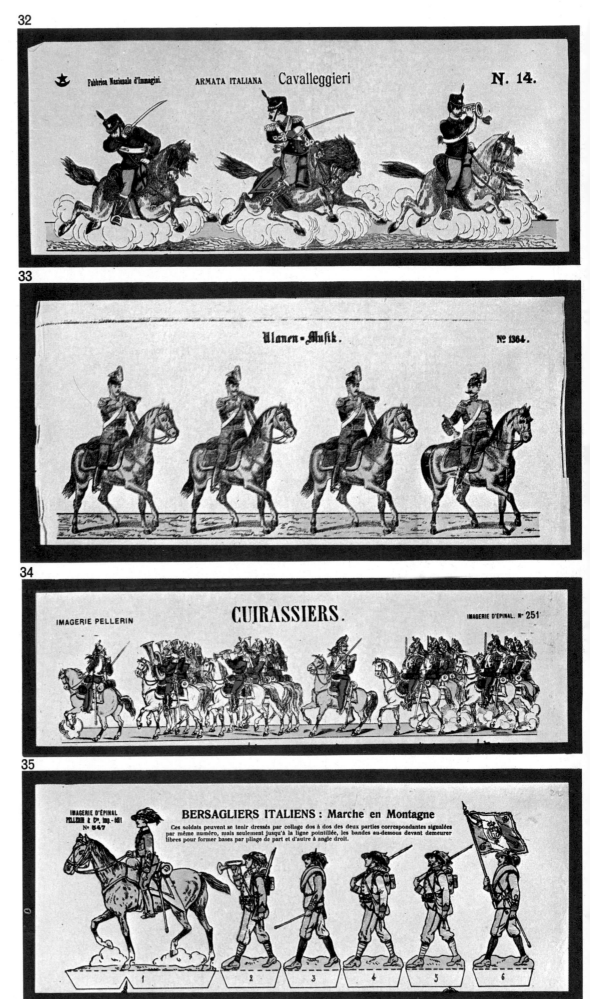

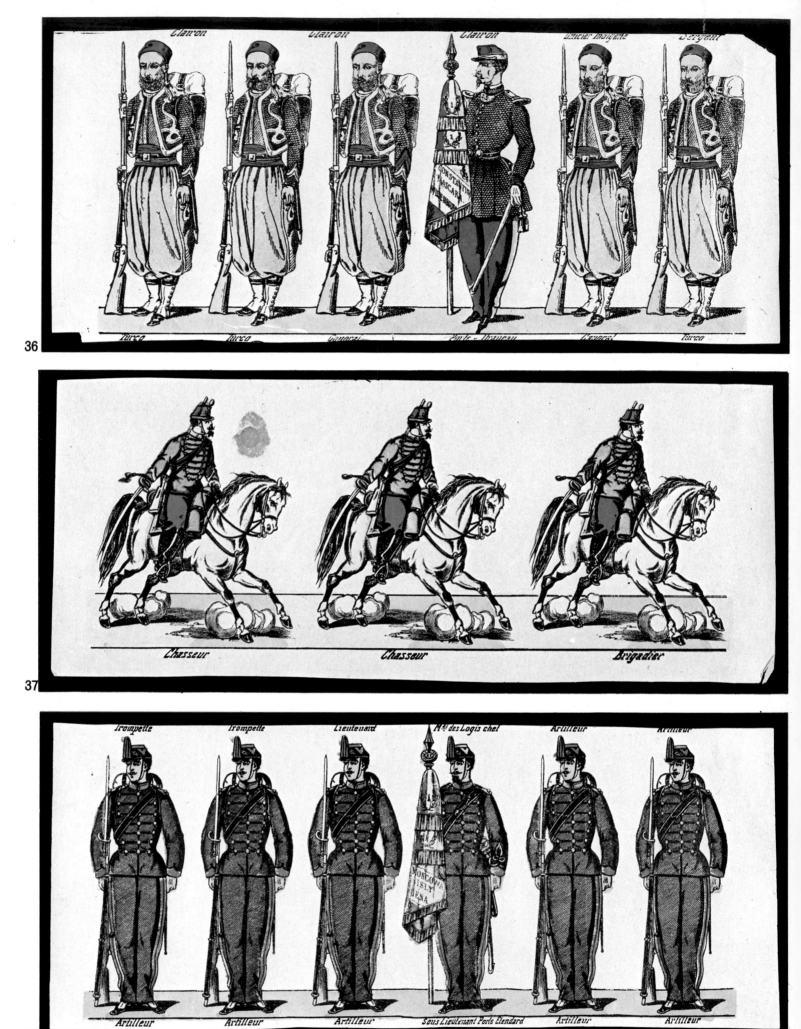

**36-38** Three more selections from the enormous range of uniform prints by Pellerin of Epinal.

**36** French colonial troops from North Africa, of the time of Napoleon III's Second Empire: a colour-bearer and five 'Turcos'.

**37** Sergeant-of-Horse and two troopers of the *élite* Chasseurs d'Afrique, which charged in support of Lord Cardigan's Light Brigade in the Battle of Balaclava.

**38** French Second Empire artillerymen in parade order. The colour carried by the second lieutenant displays the proud battle honours of 'Moscowa' (Borodino) and 'Jena', two of Napoleon I's victories.

**39** A file of British Grenadiers, very obviously marching 'at ease'! For many years these were the only model soldiers an ordinary boy could hope to afford; printed on paper, stuck on to cardboard and cut out, and given supports to make them stand up.

39

40

**40** The 'cut-out' as a toy: at the back of each of these machine-gunners is a metal 'clicker'. When rattled, it suggests machine-gun fire. These figures both come from the Testi Collection.

**41** Also from the Testi Collection come these rough, crudely-coloured aluminium alloy figures. Nondescript as they look, they are nevertheless rare examples of model soldiers made in the USSR between the world wars. Presumably they represent Red Guards of the Revolution, although the machine-gun on its small, two-wheeled trolley was a type used in both the First and Second World Wars by the Red Army.

41

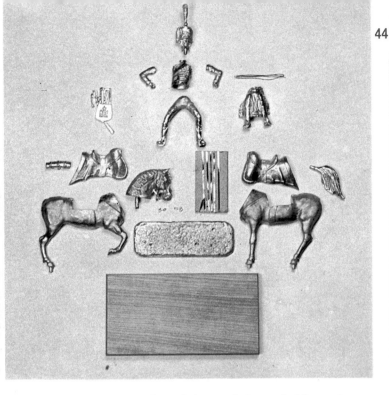

**42-43** How the box-presentation technique made famous by Mignot of Paris was applied to civilian subjects. These two offerings represent a detachment of Parisian firemen with their equipment, and scenes from the American explorer Peary's arduous journey to the North Pole in 1909. The presentation of these toys draws attention to two important criteria which have always obsessed the makers and collectors of far more sophisticated model soldiers: concern with detail, and as realistic a display as possible.

**44-47** These four plates show the genesis of an Imrie-Risley model soldier. Photographed by Philip Stearns, they show the metal components of the original kit, the assembled model, the assembled model with its undercoat of paint, and the completed figure, perfect in detail down to the last harness buckle and tunic button.

**48-49** Of these modern Mignot figures, some have been left in their original state (particularly the group of three) while others have been adapted. Here the difference between the 'toy soldier' straight from the maker and the figure intended to be a permanent showpiece is more evident. All are traditional *ronde-bosse* figures, 54 mm high, and showing different uniforms of the French Revolutionary Army of 1792.

**50** A small diorama, again from the Testi Collection, using three reworked figures: Napoleon studies his map, flanked by his Mameluke servant and a standard-bearer of Chasseurs.

**48 49**

50

51  52

**51** A grenadier of Napoleon's Old Guard accepts a pinch of snuff from his Emperor – a good example of how imaginative treatment can make model soldiers so much more than merely attractively-painted manikins. Figures by Stadden, from the collection of Peter Blum; photography by Philip Stearns.

**52** The work of the specialist: an officer of Napoleon's *Grenadiers à Cheval* by Fernande Métayer of Paris (Alberini Collection). This specimen could never be thought of as a mere toy. Madame Métayer belongs to that group of French artists which 'discovered' the specialist-made military miniature during the Second World War. Some of these craftsmen were unemployed goldsmiths and jewellers; some were people who, confined to their homes, did not know what to do to earn money. In the beginning these new makers were content to modify the mass-produced models of Mignot and others, using the small welding lamps used by goldsmiths and carefully painting each specimen; soon there was an increasing demand for original individual figures made to the highest possible standards. Now a horse and rider would be cast separately; cloaks and other accoutrements would be created piece by piece and added to the figure, with the same applying to horse furniture and weapons. For an artist it soon became a point of honour that each figure should be completely accurate in detail, right down to the last gaiter-button.

53  54

**53** This is a small but attractive diorama from Norman Newton Ltd. It shows a patrol of German infantrymen of 1914–15 (the distinctive German 'coal-scuttle' helmet was not issued until 1916). The figures are Stadden.

**54** The work of Eugène Leliepvre: a French dragoon of the seventeenth century literally 'correct to the last stitch'. The uniform is made of cloth, and is stitched along the seams of the original garments. To succeed with this sort of detail it is necessary to work on a larger figure than the standard miniature size. In this case, man and horse together stand 16 inches tall. Photographed by Philip Stearns.

**55** French fighting patrol, 1914 – a memory of the disastrous opening months of the First World War when the French Army advanced chest-high to the guns in the ludicrously conspicuous red breeches and blue coat of the Second Empire. This is a small diorama of Stadden figures, reproduced by courtesy of Norman Newton Ltd.

55

**56** The Testi Collection is particularly helpful in making the distinction between what are obviously toys and what are collectors' items. Testi collected the greatest possible number of 'childish' items, but he arranged and displayed them so as to remove any impression of impermanence, of something intended only for the moment, which toys always have. Here Genoese cavalry of the eighteenth century (*Dragons Bleus*) have been set out in one of the Collection's dioramas. The figures are by Antonini of Rome.

**57** Another diorama in the Testi Collection, devoted to the French Army of the early eighteenth century, showing a detachment of Guards and a cavalry patrol from the Balthazar Regiment. These are Mignot 'mass produced' models, not singly made, as true collectors' pieces are. One can see that the inspiration for the pose of the officer's horse was drawn from baroque monuments, at the expense of sacrificing the solidity and equilibrium of the model soldier-toy.

58

59

**58-60** Three more dioramas from the Testi Collection, showing the tendency of this collection to use simple, toylike figures for an impressive effect. *Above:* An episode from the Russo-Japanese War of 1904 – an exchange of fire between Japanese infantry and Tsarist troops, whose white dress uniforms are still in evidence even in the field. *Centre:* The Royal Spanish Artillery of about 1910. *Below:* A detachment of Spanish lancers of the same period, in their winter uniform. Although Spain's limited military activity in the twentieth century would not suggest that there would be much interest in model soldiers in that country, some very interesting work is being done there. Most worthy of mention is the firm of Aylmer at Burjasot, near Valencia. Aylmer manufactures HO Scale soldiers (1:86 scale, average height 20 mm). These *miniploms*, as they are known, permit the collector to assemble large collections of model soldiers from all over the world and of all periods. They are usually sold in tough plastic boxes in lines of four figures.

**61-62** These Testi Collection dioramas come from the 'troops on parade' series. In this case the salute is being taken by Kaiser Wilhelm II in Berlin on the eve of the First World War, with modern German models being used. *Above:* A cuirassier and a dragoon before the Brandenburg Gate. *Centre:* A detachment of cuirassiers during the march-past.

**63** Another good example of the use of 'toy' soldiers to create a non-toylike appearance when displayed in a diorama. This representation of a French airfield during the early stages of the First World War uses pre-1914 Mignot figures; the dispatch-rider is clearly a modification of the mould which produced the bicyclist-fireman in the box-diorama on page 34.

61
62

63

64

65

**64** General Ulysses Grant at Vicksburg, in a diorama from the Testi Collection. In the collector's catalogue these figures are described as English figures, and they are probably current pieces by Britain adapted for the Collection. The American Civil War has become a very popular subject, especially because of the interest in military miniatures in the United States. There are several large associations of enthusiasts in the USA, each of which publishes its own journal. And there are shops specialising in military collecting (not only model soldiers, but also uniforms, weapons and prints) such as The Soldier Shop in New York, which publishes an annual catalogue of more than 200 pages.

**65** A standard bearer of the Union Army and a Confederate trooper, from the Testi Collection. Although the production of military miniatures started very late in the United States, at the end of the nineteenth century, American manufacturers have quickly made up for lost time. One of the most famous names, although it only appeared on the market in 1938, is Comet, which merged with the Swedish firm of Ericksson after the Second World War. The catalogue of The Soldier Shop devotes many pages to the miniatures of Imrie-Risley, who specialise in the uniforms of the War of American Independence (one can order the same basic figure in 54 different poses, 33 of which are devoted to the positions of musket drill). Another popular subject well exploited by Imrie-Risley is the American Civil War.

**66** General Robert E. Lee of the Confederate Army of Northern Virginia with his staff at the Battle of Gettysburg. These are Imrie-Risley figures, with special out-of-door photography by Philip Stearns.

**67** Union cavalry fight a dismounted action in the opening stages of the Battle of Gettysburg in 1863. These are Imrie-Risley figures, enhanced with out-of-door photography by Philip Stearns.

68

69  70

**68** One of the most exquisite models ever made, and the perfect answer to the sceptic who dismisses model soldiers as toys. This figure started life as a jumble of plastic components in a Historex kit. It was then transformed by the animation and artistic skill of Ray Lamb to produce a three-dimensional replica, perfect in every detail, of Géricault's painting of a Chasseur of the French Imperial Guard, and it was photographed by Philip Stearns. Beautiful as it is, this figure has set a standard which few military modellers can hope to match – but those who can will do so with the express intention of raising these standards still higher. When plastic first appeared as a material for military modelling, many collectors looked askance, but after the success of Historex with their intricately detailed series of kit models (concentrating on the Grand Army of Napoleon) the advantages of modelling in plastic have been generally accepted. No matter how well these models are built up, however, the secret of an outstanding piece of work lies in the animation – and all the patience devoted to the model can still be totally wasted by a careless or inaccurate painting job. The goal remains perfection.

**69-70** Artillery of Washington's Patriot Army in the field during the War of American Independence. These are Imrie-Risley figures from the collection of Peter Blum, with out-of-door photography by Philip Stearns.

**71** The ring of antiquity: Pharaoh Thut-Mose III rides into battle in his war chariot. These figures are by Russell Gammage, mounted and painted by Donald Burgess for the collection of Philip Stearns, who also photographed them.

**72** Magnificent portrait figures of George Washington and the Marquis de Lafayette, by Mademoiselle Josiane Desfontaines. Washington and Lafayette are depicted at the siege of Yorktown in 1781, the battle which clinched the British defeat in the American War of Independence. The impressive detail of these figures is particularly interesting: the uniforms were made from thin metal sheeting, cut and folded as if it were cloth, with the buttons added later. These figures are from the collection of Peter Blum, with out-of-door photography by Philip Stearns.

**73-75** The work of Gianni Tura of Milan, who considers the subject purely as a hobby, must certainly be included here. His work is entirely free of commercial motives: it is only very rarely that he will sell one of his models. Tura works only in plastic, modifying commercial prototypes or rough models – particularly those of Almerk, an English firm which sells 54-mm plastic models ideally suited for this sort of work. The subjects which made Tura known to collectors were Japanese Samurai; his models became known during studies on medieval Japanese militaria which were published in Holland. *Above:* Two thirteenth century warriors in four-plate armour, simulated by overlaying flexible sheets of plastic on the basic model (in this case, one of the Duke of Wellington). *Below:* This sixteenth-century Samurai's armour has a greater number of plates; the flag, already adopted by that date, shows that he belongs to a clan. Each of these models needs an average of twenty hours' work, excluding research.

**76** Japanese infantry patrol of the Second World War. The officer brandishes his Samurai sword. Tura makes the weapons for his soldiers from wood, all of them faithful to their originals.

**77** A twelfth-century Norman knight in chain mail contrived from a section of a nylon stocking, lightly varnished! Tura's basic figure was a seventeenth-century grenadier by Britain. The shield required very delicate work: it was made from a printed wooden mould on to which was pressed a piece of plastic, heated to make it malleable. The blazon on the shield was taken from a design on the Bayeux Tapestry.

**78** A German motorcyclist on the Russian Front, 1941. The basic model was a dispatch rider made by Britain. It is mounted on a completely reworked model of a BMW motorcycle. Tura has also added goggles, gauntlets, weapons, and carefully textured Russian 'mud'.

**79** Another masterpiece of Eugène Leliepvre, this time a French hussar of the *ancien régime*. The details of the model's equipment are as faithful as those of the dragoon. Photographed by Philip Stearns.

**80-81** Two more 54-mm figures by Gianni Tura: an Italian infantryman of 1917 in battle order, complete with cape, and a French *Chasseur Alpin*, from that famous regiment of mountain troops also known as the 'Blue Devils'. Tura prefers to try and capture the basic appearance of the soldier he is modelling without undue concern with superfluous detail. Here he differs considerably from the majority of military modellers, but his figures certainly have an appeal of their own.

79

80

82

83

**82-83** French guards of 1742, from the Noé Collection, of unknown Spanish manufacture. These are also 54-mm figures.

**84** A volunteer of the Spanish Crown, 1796, from the Noé Collection. These models show the impressive standard reached today by Spanish makers of lead soldiers, particularly in the traditional 54-mm *ronde-bosse*.

84

85

86

87

**85** Again from the Noé Collection: a small framed diorama. The figure of Napoleon is a reworked 54-mm model and the horse has a tail made of horsehair. According to the owner it was made about twenty years ago.

**86** A French general of about 1860, of the Army of Napoleon III's Second Empire. It is a good piece of work from Rose Models by Russell Gammage, one of the best contemporary English miniaturists. The execution is extremely accurate: even the sword knots on the sabre are of lead, and there is a microscopic replica of the medal of the *Légion d'Honneur*. Russell Gammage is highly praised by the experts for the quality of his castings: many craftsmen and collector-makers of model soldiers buy Rose models, either complete figures to rework or separate components (bodies, heads, arms, legs, weapons and equipment).

**87** Another 'informal pose' – a Roman legionary in marching order, and obviously fully experienced in living off the country! The figure is by William Murray, photographed by Philip Stearns.

88

**88** A close-up of Marshal Bessières, one of Napoleon's Marshals. This is a Stadden figure, and it shows how much detail and expression can be worked into a 54-mm miniature. The Marshal, from the collection of J. Linen, was photographed by Philip Stearns.

**89** A historical scene from the Testi Collection: a Prussian officer (*left*) greets a British officer on the battlefield of Waterloo after the arrival of Blücher's Prussian Army turned the day in favour of the Allies. Since each officer still holds his sabre in his right hand, they are shaking hands with their left hands. These are figures by another famous name in English modelling: Charles C. Stadden. He started producing model soldiers after the Second World War. His first figures appeared in 1951: 39 mm high at first, then 33 mm. Finally he was 'converted' to the 54-mm size, handing over the distribution of his models to Norman Newton Ltd. The Stadden catalogue is divided into three parts: miniatures (33 mm), standard (54 mm), and 'Stadden Super Statuettes'. Stadden produced two specialities: British soldiers of the Napoleonic period and regiments of the Indian Army of the late nineteenth century (Skinner's Horse, Bengal Lancers, etc.). He works principally in lead. The 'Supers' are accompanied by a certificate of guarantee which assures the uniform's fidelity to the original.

**90**

**90-93** Four figures from the Renato Artesi Collection devoted to the Italian Cavalry.

**90** Officer of the Piacenza Hussars in dress uniform, 1865.

**91** Colonel commanding the Genoese Cavalry in dress uniform, 1905

**92** Trumpeter of the Savoy Cavalry, 1930.

**93** Standard-bearer of the Savoy Cavalry during the Russian campaign of 1942.

All these figures are single pieces made by Augusto Pranzetti of Sassari. He works in wood and plaster, with additional details in cloth and leather. Sometimes he makes models from the Historex range of plastic models. Pranzetti specialises in two sizes: the traditional 54 mm (as in the four illustrated here) and 120 mm, models which more nearly resemble statuettes. Renato Artesi is not a collector of model soldiers (except for a very few specimens which have a particular interest), but in his house in Milan he has assembled one of the most important collections of militaria in Italy which is a source of reference for models, illustrations and sketches.

**91**

**94-95** Superb examples of the work of Lucien Rousselot: a French cuirassier or armoured heavy cavalryman of Napoleon's Grand Army, seen below in the setting of a miniature armoury. The detail here is amazing. The mounted figure itself stands 16 inches tall. Breastplates and helmets have been hammered out of steel. The buckles of the straps unfasten. The sabres can be drawn from their scabbards. Even the trigger mechanisms of the muskets operates. Photographed by Philip Stearns.

**96** Despite their defeat in the War of American Independence, the British could derive some satisfaction from the successes of their cavalry under the leadership of commanders such as Sir Banastre Tarleton. This figure represents one of the 17th Light Dragoons under Tarleton's command. The figure itself is by Imrie-Risley of New York, with out-of-doors photography by Philip Stearns.

94

95

**97** A group of Greek warriors of the Trojan Wars, made in plastic by Herald Models.

**98** Medieval warriors in plastic. These are *Swoppets*, another British make, which can be completely dismantled.

**99** A clash between German pikemen made in plastic by Elastolin. All the models on this page are made to the standard size of 54 mm. The pioneer of plastic model soldiers was a German, Hausser, who founded Elastolin in 1936, still a trade mark of great prestige on the world market. Destroyed by bombing during the Second World War, the Elastolin factory was back in business and was highly praised after a visit by the Control Commission in the English Sector of the Occupied Zone. Elastolin made its mark in the 1950s with its coverage of a subject immediately attractive to children: Cowboys and Indians and life in the Wild West. Thanks to the Western movie a small boy who may know little of his own country's history will know all about General Custer and the 7th Cavalry, Davy Crockett, Sitting Bull and others (oddly enough Buffalo Bill, the hero of 1910 readers, never seems to have caught on since 1945). But the real triumph of plastic models is due to English makers, most notably Herald and Britain, two major manufacturers who are now amalgamated.

100

**100** 'Napoleon' 12-pounder Confederate artillery crew of the American Civil War: plastic, with a metal barrel, total length 15 inches. When produced with blue instead of grey uniforms, it becomes a Union gun team. The model can be unlimbered as if for firing and rounded off with four artillery foot soldiers.

**101** Also by Britain: a 32-pounder naval carronade (with simulated 'bronze' barrel), with the rammer and captain of its gun crew.

101

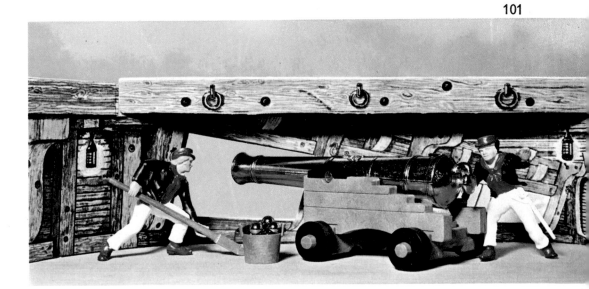

102

103

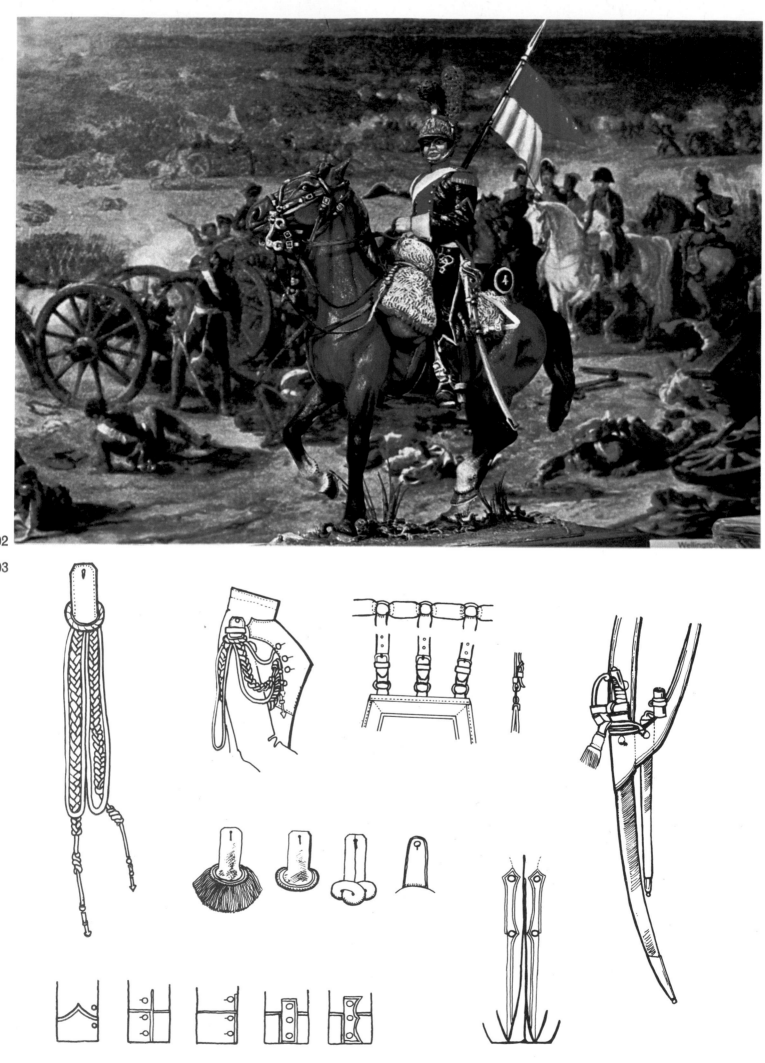

104

105

**102** French lancer of Napoleon's Grand Army. The amazing detail of the uniform blends well with the contemporary Napoleonic battle scene used as a back-drop in this pose. Courtesy Historex Agents, Dover.

**103** Details from the Historex catalogue show the variety of detail which must be faithfully reproduced in an accurate military model. Reading from left to right, they include the *aiguillette* and how it is suspended from shoulder-strap and tunic buttons; the three-ring attachment for a *sabretache*; four shoulder-strap variants (*epaulette*, *contre-epaulette*, *trefle*, and plain *patte d'épaule*); five cuff variants (*pointu*, *ouvert dessus*, *ouvert dessous*, *droite*, and *en accolade*); tunic braiding *à la Soubise*; and the combined sword and bayonet frog as worn by the French infantry of the Napoleonic Wars. Courtesy Historex Agents, Dover.

**104** Joachim Murat, King of Naples – Napoleon's flamboyant cavalry leader – with an aide. These are Historex figures, specially animated and painted by Pierre Conrad, and photographed by Philip Stearns.

**105** Another good example of how clever animation can transform a static model into the centrepiece of an amusing scene. In this case it is a Historex French lancer (by courtesy of Historex Agents).

**106** 'Trick' photography by Philip Stearns creates the impression of a mass charge. Edward Surén supplied four camel-mounted model soldiers; the photographer's skill did the rest.

**107** French and British colonial forces clash at Ticonderoga in 1759. This diorama was created by Edward Surén and photographed by Philip Stearns. It is perfect in detail, right down to the construction of the gabions – tall wicker baskets packed with earth and ranged side by side to form a breastwork or to buttress a trench.

**108** An early stage in a war game. This one deals with the mounting of an amphibious landing, which at this stage of the game is just going in. Tank and infantry landing craft have already hit the beach; stores are being unloaded, and supports are moving in from the invasion fleet 'out at sea'. It seems a somewhat one-sided battle at present – but when the Allies landed at Anzio in 1944 they took the Germans completely by surprise, the resulting German counterattack producing one of the most hard-fought battles of the Second World War. A war game to re-enact Anzio might be a faithful re-enaction of the battle as it actually happened; but it might just as easily be fought out on different lines, according to particular 'given situations' agreed between the contestants and the umpire before the first move is made. Everything possible is done to translate the realities of the battlefield into the movements of the models on the war game table; there are even 'morale' dice throws to judge whether or not the morale of troops will suffer when, for example, their officers get 'killed'. War games have played a vital role in the preparation for actual warfare. One of the best examples occurred in 1942 when the Japanese were planning to take Midway Island. The Japanese played out a war game in which the 'Japanese' carrier fleet was caught with its aircraft refuelling on deck by an 'American' air attack, causing two Japanese carriers to be 'sunk'. To save face, the umpire over-ruled the situation on the table and the game resulted in a Japanese 'victory'. But in the actual Battle of Midway (4 June 1942) the possibility suggested by that war game became reality: the Japanese lost all four of their carriers, the battle, and – as events turned out – their naval supremacy in the Pacific theatre of war.

109

**109-110** Two more magnificent battle dioramas by Edward Surén, with photography by Philip Stearns. In the top picture, Marshal Ney's heavy cavalry charges the British in the Battle of Quatre-Bras, the curtain-raiser to Waterloo in the 1815 campaign. Below, the hard-pressed British defenders of Rorke's Drift fight off a Zulu attack in the war of 1879. The Rorke's Drift diorama is currently on display in the National Army Museum in London.

Both these plates could be mistaken for historical film 'stills'. Skilfully conceived and executed dioramas such as these show not only that modern-day collectors of model soldiers are masters of their subject and base their work on exhaustive historical research: they also demonstrate that what is so often dismissed as a hobby fit only for children has become a fascinating and extremely demanding art form in its own right.

110